Sublime Blue

Sublime Blue

SELECTED EARLY ODES

OF

PABLO NERUDA

Translated and introduced
by William Pitt Root

WingsPress

San Antonio, Texas

2013

Sublime Blue: Selected Early Odes of Pablo Neruda
© 2013 by Wings Press
All Spanish texts from *Odas elementales* © 1954 by Pablo Neruda.
All English translations © 2013 by William Pitt Root.
Cover: Mendocino Coastline. Photograph by William Pitt Root.

First Edition:
Print Edition ISBN: 978-0-916727-87-1
ePub ISBN: 978-1-60940-195-5
Kindle ISBN: 978-1-60940-196-2
Library PDF ISBN: 978-1-60940-197-9

Wings Press
627 E. Guenther
San Antonio, Texas 78210
Phone/fax: (210) 271-7805
On-line catalogue and ordering:
www.wingspress.com
All Wings Press titles are distributed to the trade by
Independent Publishers Group
www.ipgbook.com

Library of Congress Cataloging-in-Publication Data:

Neruda, Pablo, 1904-1973.
  Sublime Blue : SELECTED EARLY ODES OF PABLO
NERUDA / Pablo Neruda ; Translated by William Pitt Root. -- First
Edition.
       pages cm
  This is an English translation of the Spanish texts from Odas ele-
mentales © 1954 by Pablo Neruda.
  ISBN 978-0-916727-87-1 (pbk. : alk. paper) -- ISBN 978-1-60940-
195-5 (epub ebook) -- ISBN 978-1-60940-196-2 (kindle ebook) --
ISBN 978-1-60940-197-9 (library pdf ebook)
  I. Root, William Pitt, 1941- translator. II. Neruda, Pablo, 1904-1973.
Odas elementales. III. Neruda, Pablo, 1904-1973. Odas elementales
English. IV. Title.
  PQ8097.N4O413 2013
  861'.62--dc23
                                                      2012040300

Contents

*Dedicated to Pamela,
with love, for the brilliance of her spirit
reflected in the artesian outpouring of her own odes,
and to Bryce Milligan, without whose patience
this work may never have seen the dark of
printer's ink or the light of day.*

INTRODUCTION

"OUR BREAD AND OUR DREAM"

When Neruda wrote in his *Memoirs**** that "We must open America's matrix to bring out her glorious light," he took metaphorically the *el dorado* image Cortés and company have always taken literally. In doing so, he projected a perspective which, by placing a higher value on light than on the mineral which merely imitates it, resembles the idea of gold prevalent among *las indigenas*, the first people native to the American continent. For Neruda, the poet's role as explorer was to discover and rediscover the many forms of wealth native to the spirit and to return it all mysteriously gleaming to those closest to the source.

Neruda discharged this labor unflaggingly, mining a ceaseless vein of epics, lyrics, and dramatic narratives, stopped only by his death. He died shortly after the bloody CIA-assisted coup on September 11, 1973, which toppled the popular government and ended the high promise of Salvador Allende, his close friend. Neruda's last words, according to Matilde Urrutia, his wife, were repeated over and over in his final hours: tortured by news of the brutal purge claiming the lives of Allende's friends and sympathizers, the dying poet lapsed in and out of consciousness crying, "My people, my people, what are they doing to my people!" Neruda's funeral quickly swelled to threatening proportions as his countrymen learned of his death and gathered in the streets to quote verses they knew by heart. This spontaneous convocation constituted what may be construed as the first public show of opposition to Pinochet. About that time, Pinochet's forces rerouted a small creek to flood through the poet's home, where many

---

* The *Memoirs* referred to throughout the introduction are Hardie St. Martin's translations of Neruda.

of his poems were written and stored. It is unlikely that they appreciated the profound irony of this, given the connection Neruda, throughout his life, had felt with water in all its forms.

Among North American poets, the kind of popularity excited by the man born Ricardo Eliecer Neftalí Reyes Basoalto and reborn Pablo Neruda, is quite unknown. Only in the figure of Walt Whitman, whom Neruda revered, can we find an equivalent sensibility. Both men exhibited a spirit whose passionate openheartedness readily engaged at an elemental level the issues and history of their times with the intention of making available to their contemporaries a portrait of themselves, in language close to their own speech, making them participants in a vision they could not otherwise experience so memorably.

Whitman's reception, less than a century earlier, little resembled Neruda's acclaim, which began early and lasted throughout his life. "Gossiping in the early candlelight of old age," Whitman acknowledged how "public criticism on the book and myself as author of it yet shows mark'd anger and contempt more than anything else." Now an institution, our good grey poet was first reviled as "arrogant" for proclaiming himself "the Poet of the time" and as "disgraceful" (this was the received opinion cited by Emily Dickinson to explain why she had not read her contemporary) for rooting "like a pig among a rotten garbage of licentious thoughts." Neruda, however, saw to the center of Whitman's enterprise. "I like the 'postive hero' in Walt Whitman . . . who found him without formula and brought him, not without suffering, into the intimacy of our physical life, making him share with us our bread and our dream."

Among the most prolific important poets ever to live, Neruda is, again like Whitman, one of the most widely translated poets of present times. Scores of his poems have appeared in new English translations every year since his death in 1973. The poems in this selection come from his first collection of *Odas elementales,* published in 1954, when

Neruda was about 50. Of this time he has said "nothing out of the ordinary happened to me, no adventures that would amuse my readers." Yet it was during this period that he received the Stalin Prize (later renamed the Lenin Peace Prize), and, more importantly, it was then that he and Delia del Carril "separated for good" and he moved into his new home, *La Chascona*, with Matilde Urrutia, his beloved, tempestuous, and final wife.

When Neruda began writing the odes, in 1952, he already had completed his ambitious *Residencia en la tierra* (a book he later said "breathed the rigidly pessimistic air" of the time) and, more recently, his epic *Canto general*, each a major contribution toward opening "America's matrix." So, when he turned to the odes it was, in a sense, with a heart unburdened, momentarily relieved of certain charges and free to explore experience at the simplest, most ordinary level. It was as if, reversing the chronology of Blake (whom he translated), having completed a round of songs of experience now he could embark upon these odes of innocence.

The famous, widely imitated form he chose for these poems—tall, slender poetic stalks, not unlike Queen Ann's Lace slowly rocking in a seaside breeze—brilliantly suited the air of quick spontaneity these works exude. The phrases fall like thin wrists of water cascading from great heights, exploding at intervals against ledges and obstacles protruding from a sheer cliff-face. Fluent, sinuous, riddled with delightful surprise, the offhand form is also suited to the tone of seemingly casual surmise that can so suddenly pool in a conclusion of great clarity and depth. The poet speaks of his style as a "guided spontaneity." It has also been suggested that the form derives in part from Neruda's plan to serialize these poems for newspapers whose columns, of course, are restrictively narrow.

Of his first collection of *Odas elementales* Neruda declared:

> I decided to deal with things from their beginnings, starting with the primary state, from birth onward. I

wanted to describe many things that had been sung and said over and over again. My intention was to start like the boy chewing on his pencil, setting to work on his composition assignment about the sun, the blackboard, the clock, or the family. Nothing was to be omitted from my field of action; walking or flying, I had to touch on everything, expressing myself as clearly and freshly as possible.

Elsewhere he remarked that his "tone . . . gathered strength by its own nature as time went along, like all living things."

A few odes from this and from the two subsequent collections by Neruda have become widely available to American audiences. Originally I avoided rerendering odes already familiar in order to concentrate on others less known or altogether unknown in English. In the early 80's when I began this work, only one of these odes had appeared widely in English. Twice previously this collection was accepted for publication; one publisher held the mss for years before announcing it was henceforth a printer-for-hire rather than a publisher, and the other, also after years, went bankrupt. As it happens, those delays made for a much improved set of translations. In the intervening years, other translators, including María Jacketti and Ken Krabbenhoft, have brought out collections of odes, Margaret Sayers Peden's *Selected Odes of Pablo Neruda* chief among them. Not surprisingly her collection includes versions of several more of the odes I, too, have rendered. I gladly recommend her fine work to anyone interested in the Odes, with this proviso: she has avoided altogether the more politically oriented works and such selection serves to domesticate a body of work as deliberately gnarly and behorned in some aspects as it is luminously tender in others.

I open my selection with the "The Invisible Man," which Neruda himself chose to preface his collection. (Nancy Willard has published a book-length study of this poem and its implications for modern poets and poetry.)

Here Neruda saunters familiarly first through a landscape comprised of the literary clichés of certain unnamed predecessors. He chides "my poor brother,/the poet" for his blinding degree of self-absorption and for his isolation from the "dailiness of life," to borrow from Randall Jarrell the phrase he once borrowed from a student. For Neruda, dailiness was a constant source of replenished vitality as the field of ordinary clover, rather than hothouse exotica, is sustenance to the honeybee. Then as he moves from the literary to the common world, declaring his characteristic intention to "transform [all the sorrow of the entire world] into hope" in song that reunites mankind in a spirit of celebration, he states and demonstrates a principle of self-effacement as similar in conception to Keats' "negative capability" or Eliot's annihilation of the personality as it is unlike either in execution.

In "The Invisible Man" and elsewhere, he gives us the antidote to the "I" as all-devourer and to the private ego as self-reflexive, ersatz universe, stances he regarded as essentially Romantic, defunct responses inadequate to contemporary existence. "As an active poet," Neruda recalled, "I fought against my own self-absorption and so was able to settle the debate between the real and the subjective deep within myself."

We also have here Neruda's apostrophes to the atom, to numbers, to restlessness, to hope and gloom, all general subjects paradoxically amplified by the intimacy of their rendering. Among his more intriguingly personal poems, there is his "Ode to the Unwelcome One." And in the odes to wine and the artichoke we have further evidence of his unquenchable capacity for inventive celebration. Of the blue flower also praised, his recollections from the *Memoirs* are revealing:

> Peasants and fishermen [in Chile] have forgotten the names of the small plants long ago, and the small flowers have no names now. . . . To be a hero in undiscovered territories is to be obscure; these territories and their songs

are lit only by the most anonymous blood and by flowers whose name nobody knows. Among these flowers there is one that has invaded my whole house. It's a blue flower with a long, proud, lustrous, and tough stem. At its tip, swarms of tiny infra-blue, ultra-blue flowers sway. I don't know if all human beings have the gift of seeing the sublimest blue. Is it revealed to a select few? Does it remain hidden, invisible to others? Has some blue god denied them its contemplation? Or is it only my own joy, nursed by solitude and converted into pride, gloating because it has found this blue, this blue wave, this blue star in riotous spring?

Finally, his "Ode To The Popular Poets" is yet another exploration of how the natural poet—untutored in books but instructed by the history of the vulnerable heart—can prevail upon the most painful circumstances to manifest that universal vigor "repeated in the song." Referring to certain of his fellow artists, Leonardo in his notebooks once complained of the growing tendency among aspiring artists to school themselves at the feet of their predecessors rather than in the academy of nature. He singled out as an exception Giotto, praising him for having begun his artistic career as a common shepherd sketching the objects he observed with charred sticks upon flat stones.

On the other hand, Neruda notes, "It's obvious that the poet's occupation is abused to some extent. So many new men and women poets keep cropping up that soon we'll all look like poets, and readers will disappear." The myth of the "mute, inglorious Milton" can become a conceit harboring disdain for discipline and self-discipline, as in the Elvis Presley movie "Wild In The Country," popular some decades back. For Neruda and his countrymen, the rigors of the Chilean peasants' daily lives did not include such self-aggrandizing attitudes. That life was—and is— hard, basic, perilous, joyous. Songs providing stays against despair inevitably raise the spirits of an audience. This is done not by standing outside the common lot but by sharing and reshaping it from within, much as early blues musicians, and occasional rare individuals such as Woody Guthrie, have done earlier for us in the 20th century and as indigenous musicians globally are doing for us now in this new cyber-century. Speaking of "the other family of poets" (those not nurtured by an aristocracy), Neruda fondly lists "the militant wanderers of poetry, bar lions, fascinating madmen, tormented sleepwalkers. And let's not overlook those writers tied down, like the galley slave to his oar, to the little stools in government offices."

Speaking of an earlier vatic function of poetry—"from it came liturgy, the psalms, and also the contents of religions"—, Neruda suggests an interesting transition from the function of poet as witness of nature to poet as witness of human nature:

> The poet confronted nature's phenomena and in the early ages called himself a priest, to safeguard his vocation. In the same way, to defend his poetry, the poet of the modern age accepts the investiture earned in the street, among the masses. Today's social poet is still a member of the earliest order of priests. In the old days he made his pact with the darkness, and now he must interpret the light.

Implicit in the scope and textures of Neruda's work is the challenge of a model which poets anywhere in any time, even American poets in our time, might usefully reconsider:

> The bourgeoise [Neruda warns his fellow poets] demands a poetry that is more and more isolated from reality. The poet who knows how to call a spade a spade is dangerous to a capitalism on its last legs. It is more convenient for the poet to believe himself a "small god," as Vicente Huidobro said . . . [so that] the poet basks in his own divine isolation, and there is no need to bribe or crush him. He has bribed himself by condemning himself to his heaven.

A complete poet is a complete human being—not a specialist, a technician comprehensible chiefly to fellow technicians—who works as the universe itself works, building out of elemental materials those increasingly profound structures in which may live and breathe the astonishing and mysterious varieties of the human spirit.

The model and spirit of the model are apparent and pervasive among the *Odas elementales,* where effortlessly high spirits keep close company even with grave matters.

For invaluable help in rendering these poems from Spanish, I wish to acknowledge my thanks to Junardi Armstrong of Oracle, Arizona, who went through my earliest versions of most of these poems with me years ago; to Professors Lois Welch and David Loughran of the University of Montana, who kindly offered further corrections of some of the later drafts; and to my daughter, Jennifer Lorca Root, who first helped me draft "Ode To The Blue Flower." I also wish to thank Teresa Acevedo and Juanita Melendez for help with "Ode to Poverty." And I wish especially to thank both Maria Luisa R. Lacabe of Seattle and Hedy Hebra of the Western Michigan University, who encouraged me and painstakingly annotated my versions of most of these poems with countless invaluable suggestions and corrections. Thanks also to Dave Oliphant of Austin for his invaluable last-minute suggestions, to Melissa Pritchard, who so generously and often has harbored us in the sanctuary of her Phoenix home as Pam has been courageously resurrecting herself from the ashes of her cancer. And of course, and as always, I thank my wife, the poet Pamela Uschuk, for her many helpful readings and suggestions.

I once wrote a short piece positing that "translating poetry is like trying to carry a wave in a bucket." Certainly these poems often do refer us to the sea, for a sense of what is most vital, dauntless, vast, finally reassuring. Perhaps it is apt that I first undertook to translate them in the Sonoran desert, ghost of a vast prehistoric sea. Whitman wrote of believing sea waves could be a poet's most apt mentors. Translators, perhaps, more often settle for the modest model inherent in Robert Creeley's "Be wet/with a decent happiness."

All grace notes are due to my helping hands, including, I suspect, those of *el maestro* from time to time. All errors and infelicities, as well as any demonstrations of how original wine can be converted into tap water, are entirely my own.

William Pitt Root
Oracle, Oklahoma City, Port Townsend, Missoula,
Gig Harbor, Tucson/American Airlines/Manhattan,
Winston-Salem, Knoxville, Durango

Sublime Blue

El hombre invisible

Yo me río,
me sonrío
de los viejos poetas,
yo adoro toda
la poesía escrita,
todo el rocío,
luna, diamante, gota
de plata sumergida,
que fue mi antiguo hermano,
agregando a la rosa,
pero
me sonrío
siempre dicen "yo"
a cada paso
les sucede algo,
es siempre "yo",
por las calles
sólo ellos andan
o la, dulce que aman,
nadie más,
no pasan pescadores,
ni libreros,
no pasan albañiles,
nadie se cae
de un andamio,
nadie sufre,
nadie ama,
sólo mi pobre hermano,
el poeta,
a él le pasan
todas las cosas
ya su dulce querida,
nadie vive

The Invisible Man

I laugh
and I smile
when it comes to the old poets,
I adore all
the poetry they wrote,
all the dew-
moon-diamond-drops
of sunken silver
my older brother gathered
to improve upon the rose,
yet
I smile,
for always they say "I,"
every time
something happens,
always they say "I,"
through the streets
it is only they who walk
they or the one they love,
no one else is ever around,
no fishermen pass,
no booksellers,
bricklayers never pass,
no one tumbles
from a scaffold,
no one suffers,
no one's in love,
only my poor brother,
the poet,
all things happen
to him
or to his sweet mistress,
no one else even exists,

sino él solo,
nadie llora de hambre
o de ira,
nadie sufre en sus versos
porque no puede
pagar el alquiler,
a nadie en poesía
echan a la calle
con camas y con sillas
y en las fábricas
tampoco pasa nada,
no pasa nada,
se hacen paraguas, copas,
armas, locomotoras,
se extraen minerales
rascando el infierno,
hay huelga,
vienen soldados,
disparan,
disparan contra el pueblo,
es decir,
contra la poesía,
y mi hermano
el poeta
estaba enamorado, o sufría
porque sus sentimientos
son marinos,
ama los puertos
remotos, por sus nombres,
y escribe sobre océanos
que no conoce,
junto a la vida, repleta
como el maíz de granos,
él pasa sin saber
desgranarla,
él sube y baja
sin tocar la tierra,

just him and him alone,
no one cries out in hunger
or wrath,
in his verses no one suffers
unable
make the rent,
never in his poetry
is anyone thrown out into the street
along with the bed and chairs
and in the factories
nothing happens,
not a thing,
umbrellas are made, wine glasses,
weapons, locomotives,
scraping out that hell
they extract minerals,
there's a labor strike,
soldiers come,
they shoot,
they fire against the people,
that is to say
against poetry,
and my brother
the poet
is in love, or suffers
because of his passion
for the sea,
he loves exotic ports
for their names,
he writes of oceans
he doesn't know,
he passes right alongside of life
without knowing enough
to harvest its plenty bulging
like kernels from an ear of corn,
he falls and rises
without ever touching earth,

o a veces
se siente profundísimo
y tenebroso,
él es tan grande
que no cabe en sí mismo,
se enreda y desenreda,
se declara maldito,
lleva con gran dificultad la cruz
de las tinieblas,
piensa que es diferente
a todo el mundo,
todos los días come pan
pero no ha visto nunca
un panadero
ni ha entrado a un sindicato
de panificadores,
y así mi pobre hermano
se hace oscuro,
se tuerce y se retuerce
y se halla
interesante,
interesante,
ésta es la palabra,
yo no soy superior
a mi hermano
pero sonrío,
porque voy por las calles
y sólo yo no existo,
la vida corre
como todos los ríos,
yo soy el único
invisible,
no hay misteriosas sombras,
no hay tinieblas,
todo el mundo me habla,
me quieren contar cosas,
me hablan de sus parientes,

or sometimes
he feels profoundly sad,
a melancholy
so great
his mere body can no longer contain him
so he is entangled and untangled,
declares himself cursed,
with great difficulty carries the cross
of shadows,
he believes himself unique
in all the world,
every day he eats bread
but he's never greeted
a baker
never entered a baker's union,
and so my poor brother
surrenders himself to darkness,
tortures himself,
tortures himself again
and finds himself
interesting,
interesting,
that's the word,
nor am I superior
to my brother
when I smile,
because as I go through the streets
I alone do not exist,
life runs
as all rivers run,
I am the only one
invisible,
there are no mysterious shadows,
no darkness and gloom,
everyone speaks to me,
they want to tell me things,
they talk about their relatives,

de sus miserias
y de sus alegrías,
todos pasan y todos
me dicen algo,
y cuántas cosas hacen!:
cortan maderas,
suben hilos eléctricos,
amasan hasta tarde en la noche
el pan de cada día,
con una lanza de hierro
perforan las entrañas
de la tierra
y convierten el hierro
en cerraduras,
suben al cielo y llevan
cartas, sollozos, besos,
en cada puerta hay
alguien,
nace alguno,
o me espera la que amo,
y yo paso y las cosas
me piden que las cante,
yo no tengo tiempo,
debo pensar en todo,
debo volver a casa,
pasar al Partido,
qué puedo hacer,
todo me pide
que hable,
todo me pide
que cante y cante siempre,
todo está lleno
de sueños y sonidos,
la vida es una caja
llena de cantos, se abre
y vuela y viene
una bandada

their miseries
and their joys,
everyone comes by and everyone
tells me something new,
and how many things they do!
They chop down trees,
climb up electric poles,
late into night they knead loaves
for the daily bread,
with an iron lance
they pierce the entrails
of the earth
converting the iron there
into locks,
they climb to the very heavens carrying
letters, kisses, sobs,
in each doorway
there is someone,
someone is born;
or my love waits for me,
and as I pass
all things ask me to sing
about them,
I don't have time,
I should be mindful of everything,
I should go home,
should pass by the Party office,
but what can I do,
everything calls out
for me to speak,
everything asks me
to sing and sing forever,
everything brims
with dreams and sounds,
life is a box
full of songs, when it opens
out flies a flock

de pájaros
que quieren contarme
algo descansando en mis hombros,
la vida es una lucha
como un río que avanza
y los hombres
quieren decirme,
decirte,
por qué luchan,
si mueren,
por qué mueren,
y yo paso y no tengo
tiempo para tantas vidas,
yo quiero
que todos vivan
en mi vida
y canten en mi canto,
yo no tengo importancia,
no tengo tiempo
para mis asuntos,
de noche y de día
debo anotar lo que pasa,
y no olvidar a nadie.
Es verdad que de pronto
me fatigo
y miro las estrellas,
me tiendo en el pasto, pasa
un insecto color de violín,
pongo el brazo
sobre un pequeño seno
o bajo la cintura
de la dulce que amo,
y miro el terciopelo duro
de la noche que tiembla
con sus constelaciones congeladas,
entonces
siento subir a mi alma

of birds
who wish to tell me something
settling on my shoulders,
life is a struggle
like a river that advances
and men
want to tell me,
to tell you
why they struggle,
and if they die
why,
and I go on by without the time
for so many lives,
I want
everyone to live
through my life
and to sing through my song,
I'm not important,
I haven't time
for my own affairs,
night and day
I must record everything,
and forget no one.
It's true that suddenly
I tire
and look up at the stars,
I lie down in the grass, an insect
the color of a violin passes by,
I put my arm
across a small breast
or under the waist
of the one I love,
and I watch the tough velvet
of night trembling
with its frozen constellations,
then
feel rising through my soul

la ola de los misterios,
la infancia,
el llanto en los rincones,
la adolescencia triste,
y me da sueño,
y duermo
como un manzano,
me quedo dormido
de inmediato
con las estrellas o sin las estrellas,
con mi amor o sin ella,
y cuando me levanto
se fue la noche,
la calle ha despertado antes que yo,
a su trabajo
van las muchachas pobres,
los pescadores vuelven
del océano,
los mineros
van con zapatos nuevos
entrando en la mina,
todo vive,
todos pasan,
andan apresurados,
y yo tengo apenas tiempo
para vestirme,
yo tengo que correr:
ninguno puede
pasar sin que yo sepa
adónde va, qué cosa
le ha sucedido.
No puedo
sin la vida vivir,
sin el hombre ser hombre
y corro y veo y oigo
y canto,
las estrellas no tienen

the wave of mysteries,
of childhood,
the weeping in corners,
the sad adolescence,
and it makes me sleepy
and I sleep
like an apple tree,
immediately
I am sleeping gently
with the stars or without them,
with my love or without her,
and when I rise
night has gone,
the street has awakened before me,
the poor young women
are heading for work,
the fishermen returning
from the ocean,
the miners
with their new shoes
are entering the mine,
everything's alive,
everyone's passing by,
they walk by quickly,
and I scarcely have time
to dress,
I have to run:
no one should
pass without my knowing
where he goes, what
he does.
I cannot
live without life,
be a man without mankind
and I hurry and I hear and I see
and I sing,
for the stars

nada que ver conmigo,
la soledad no tiene
flor ni fruto.
Dadme para mi vida
todas las vidas,
dadme todo el dolor
de todo el mundo,
yo voy a transformarlo
en esperanza.
Dadme
todas las alegrías,
aun las más secretas,
porque si así no fuera,
cómo van a saberse?
Yo tengo que contarlas,
dadme
las luchas
de cada día
porque ellas son mi canto,
y así andaremos juntos,
codo a codo,
todos los hombres,
mi canto los reúne:
el canto del hombre invisible
que canta con todos los hombres.

have nothing to do with me,
solitude bears neither
flower nor fruit.
Give me for my life
all lives,
give me all the sorrow
of the whole world,
I will transform it
into hope.
Give me
all joys,
even the most intimate,
otherwise
how shall they be known?
I have to speak of them,
give me
the struggles of
each day
because they are my song,
and so we will walk together,
elbow to elbow,
all mankind,
my song reunites them:
song of the invisible man
who sings with all mankind.

Oda a la alcachofa

La alcachofa
de tierno corazón
se vistió de guerrero,
erecta, construyó
una pequeña cúpula,
se mantuvo
impermeable
bajo
sus escamas,
a su lado
los vegetales locos
se encresparon,
se hicieron
zarcillos, espadañas,
bulbos conmovedores,
en el subsuelo
durmió la zanahoria
de bigotes rojos,
la viña
resecó los sarmientos
por donde sube el vino,
la col
se dedicó
a probarse faldas,
el orégano
a perfumar el mundo,
y la dulce
alcachofa
allí en el huerto,
vestida de guerrero,
bruñida
como una granada,
orgullosa,

Ode to the Artichoke

The tender-hearted
upright
artichoke
girded itself as
a warrior, constructed
a small dome,
to keep itself
waterproof
within
its scales.
At its side
crazy vegetables
ruffled up
in cat-tails and tendrils,
bulbs on the march;
underground
slept
the red-whiskered carrot,
the vineyard
withered the shoots
wine once rose through,
the cabbage
devoted itself
to trying on skirts,
oregano
scented the world,
and right there in the garden
the meek
artichoke,
girded for battle,
burnished
as a grenade,
haughty,

y un día
una con otra
en grandes cestos
de mimbre, caminó
por el mercado
a realizar su sueño:
la milicia.
En hileras
nunca fue tan marcial
como en la feria,
los hombres
entre las legumbres
con sus camisas blancas
eran
mariscales
de las alcachofas,
las filas apretadas,
las voces de comando,
y la detonación
de una caja que cae,
pero
entonces
viene
María
con su cesto,
escoge
una alcachofa,
no le teme,
la examina, la observa
contra la luz como si fuera un huevo,
la compra,
la confunde
en su bolsa
con un par de zapatos,
con un repollo y una
botella

and then one day
it was into the grand
willow basket
with the others and off
to the market
it marched
to fulfill its dream:
the militia!
In columns
never more martial
than at the fair,
men
in their white shirts
among the vegetables
became
field marshals
of the artichokes,
the closed ranks,
the voices of command,
and the sudden detonation
of . . . a fumbled cashbox,
but
then
comes
Maria
with her basket,
who fearlessly
picks out
an artichoke,
looking at it, examining it
against the light as if it were an egg,
she buys it,
drops it
into her basket
with a pair of shoes,
a white cabbage and a
bottle

de vinagre
hasta
que entrando a la cocina
la sumerge en la olla.
Así termina
en paz
esta carrera
del vegetal armado
que se llama alcachofa,
luego
escama por escama
desvestimos
la delicia
y comemos
la pacífica pasta
de su corazón verde.

of vinegar as well
then
entering the kitchen
plunges it into the pot.
And so it ends,
in peace,
the career
of the armored vegetable
called "artichoke,"
and presently
scale by scale
we undress
this delight
we munch
the peaceful paste
of its green heart.

Oda al átomo

Pequeñísima
estrella,
parecías
para siempre
enterrada
en el metal: oculto,
tu diabólico
fuego.
Un día golpearon
en la puerta
minúscula:
era el hombre.
Con una descarga
te desencadenaron,
viste el mundo,
saliste
por el día,
recorriste
ciudades,
tu gran fulgor llegaba
a iluminar las vidas,
eras
una fruta terrible,
de eléctrica hermosura,
venías
a apresurar las llamas
del estío,
y entonces
llegó
armado
con anteojos de tigre
y armadura,
con camisa cuadrada,

Ode to the Atom

Infinitesmal
star, within
the metal
you appeared
to be interred
forever: concealed,
your diabolical
fire.
Then one day
loud knocking
at the tiny door:
it was man.
With a burst
you were unbound,
you saw the world,
came out
into daylight,
scanning
cities,
your great radiance arriving
to light our lives;
you were
a terrible fruit,
of electric beauty,
and you came
to fan the flames
of summer,
but then
he arrived
armed
with the binocular eyes of the tiger
and armor,
with pleated shirts and

sulfúricos bigotes,
cola de puerco espín,
llegó el guerrero
y te sedujo:
duerme,
te dijo,
enróllate,
átomo, te pareces
a un dios griego,
a una primaveral
modista de París,
acuéstate
en mi uña,
entra en esta cajita,
y entonces
el guerrero
te guardó en su chaleco
como si fueras sólo
píldora
norteamericana,
y viajó por el mundo
dejándote caer
en Hiroshima.

Despertamos.

La aurora
se había consumido.
Todos los pájaros
cayeron calcinados.
Un olor
de ataúd,
gas de las tumbas,
tronó por los espacios.
Subió horrenda
la forma del castigo
sobrehumano,

sulphurous mustaches
and the tail of a porcupine,
the warrior came
and seduced you:
"Sleep,"
he told you, "Roll up, atom,
you look like
a Greek god,
bright as a
Parisian *modiste.*
Now curl up,
lie down
on my fingernail,
slip into this tiny box."
And then
the warrior
guarded you in his vest pocket
as if you were only
some pill
from North America,
and he traveled the world
letting you drop
on Hiroshima.

We awaken.

Dawn
had been devoured.
All the birds
fell charred.
The stench
of coffins,
entombed gasses
thundered everywhere through space.
Uprose, the horrendous
form of
superhuman punishment

hongo sangriento, cúpula,
humareda,
espada
del infierno.
Subió quemante el aire
y se esparció la muerte
en ondas paralelas,
alcanzando
a la madre dormida
con su niño,
al pescador del río
y a los peces,
a la panadería
y a los panes,
al ingeniero
y a sus edificios,
todo
fue polvo
que mordía,
aire
asesino.

La ciudad
desmoronó sus últimos alvéolos,
cayó, cayó de pronto,
derribada,
podrida,
los hombres
fueron súbitos leprosos,
tomaban
la mano de sus hijos
y la pequeña mano
se quedaba en sus manos.
Así, de tu refugio,
del secreto
manto de piedra
en que el fuego dormía

uprose—bloodbright mushroom dome,
smoldering cloud,
sword
from the abyssal inferno,
its ascent searing air.
And death spread out
in those parallel waves,
reaching
the mother asleep with her child,
the fisherman at the river
and the fishes,
the baker
and the loaves,
the engineer
and his buildings,
everything
was acidic
dust,
assassin
air.

Like a lung the city collapsed,
in its farthest alveoles
it fell, abruptly
overthrown and
corrupt,
the men there suddenly
leprous so that as they
reached for the hands of their sons
those little hands
came off in their own.
And so it was,
blinding spark,
rabid light,
that they drew you out
from your refuge
in the secret mantle of stone

te sacaron,
chispa enceguecedora,
luz rabiosa,
a destruir las vidas,
a perseguir lejanas existencias,
bajo el mar,
en el aire,
en las arenas,
en el último
recodo de los puertos,
a borrar
las semillas,
a asesinar los gérmenes,
a impedir la corola,
te destinaron, átomo,
a dejar arrasadas
las naciones,
a convertir el amor en negra pústula,
a quemar amontonados corazones
y aniquilar la sangre.

Oh chispa loca,
vuelve
a tu mortaja,
entiérrate
en tus mantos minerales,
vuelve a ser piedra ciega,
desoye a los bandidos,
colabora
tú, con la vida, con la agricultura,
suplanta los motores,
eleva la energía,
fecunda los planetas.
Ya no tienes
secreto,
camina
entre los hombres

where the fire slept—
to destroy lives,
to pursue creatures remote
beneath the sea,
in the air,
on the deserts,
in the crooks
of the farthest ports,
to erase seeds,
annihilate spores
and block corollas,
they designated you,
Atom,
to level nations
and convert love into a black pustule,
to incinerate the heaped-up hearts
and obliterate
their blood.

Oh lunatic spark,
go back
to your shroud,
bury yourself
in your mineral robes,
return to being blind stone,
deafen yourself to such criminals;
involve yourself, yes,
but with life, with agriculture,
replace engines,
increase our energy
and vitalize the planets.
You have no
secret
and can walk
among men

sin máscara
apresurando el paso
y extendiendo
los pasos de los frutos,
separando
montañas,
enderezando ríos,
fecundando,
átomo,
desbordada
copa
cósmica,
vuelve
a la paz del racimo,
a la velocidad de la alegría,
vuelve al recinto
de la naturaleza,
ponte a nuestro servicio,
y en vez de las cenizas
mortales
de tu máscara,
en vez de los infiernos desatados
de tu cólera,
en vez de la amenaza
de tu terrible claridad, entréganos
tu sobrecogedora
rebeldía
para los cereales,
tu magnetismo desencadenado
para fundar la paz entre los hombres,
y así no será infierno
tu luz deslumbradora,
sino felicidad,
matutina esperanza,
contribución terrestre.

without mascarade,
speeding your progress
and extending
the seasons for fruits,
cleaving
mountains,
straightening out rivers,
fertilizing
and overflowing
the cosmic
cup,
Atom,
return
to the tranquility of the cluster
and the velocity of joy,
return to the confines
of nature,
and put yourself at our service,
and instead of the fatal
ashes
of your mask,
instead of the unleashed infernos
of your wrath,
instead of the menace
of your terrible brilliance,
surrender to us your astonishing
defiance
that it may increase the harvests,
your unbound magnetism
to establish peace among men,
and then the dazzle
of your light will be
not hell,
but happiness,
hope for dawn,
an earthly charity.

Oda a la esperanza

Crepúsculo marino,
en medio
de mi vida,
las olas como uvas,
la soledad del cielo,
me llenas
y desbordas,
todo el mar,
todo el cielo,
movimiento
y espacio,
los batallones blancos
de la espuma,
la tierra anaranjada,
la cintura
incendiada
del sol en agonía,
tantos
dones y dones,
aves
que acuden a sus sueños,
y el mar, el mar,
aroma
suspendido,
coro de sal sonora,
mientras tanto,
nosotros,
los hombres,
junto al agua,
luchando
y esperando,

Ode to Hope

Marine twilight,
in the middle of
my life,
the waves like clustered grapes,
the solitude of the sky,
full you
overflow in me,
all the sea,
all the sky,
motion
and space,
the white legions
of foam,
orange land
and the burning
waist of
the sun in agony
after so much giving
and giving,
birds
who rush to their own dreams,
and the sea, the sea,
the suspended
scent,
the melodious choiring of salt;
meanwhile
we
men
join along with the water,
hoping
and striving

junto al mar,
esperando.
Las olas dicen a la costa firme:
"Todo será cumplido".

by the sea,
hoping.
Waves whisper to the solid coast:
"All will be made whole."

Oda a la flor azul

Caminando hacia el mar
en la pradera
— es hoy noviembre —
todo ha nacido ya,
todo tiene estatura,
ondulación, fragrancia.
Hierba a hierba
entenderé la tierra,
paso a paso
hasta la línea loca
del océano.
De pronto una ola
de aire agita y ondula
la cebada salvaje:
salta
el vuelo de un pájaro
desde mis pies, el suelo
lleno de hilos de oro,
de pétalos sin nombre,
brilla de pronto como rosa verde,
se enreda con ortigas que revelan
su coral enemigo,
esbeltos tallos, zarzas
estrelladas,
diferencia infinita
de cada vegetal que me saluda
a veces con un rápido
centelleo de espinas
o con la pulsación de su perfume
fresco, fino y amargo.
Andando a las espumas
del Pacífico
con torpe paso por la baja hierba

Ode to the Blue Flower

Walking toward the sea
across the meadow
—it is November*—
everything's in blossom,
everything has its full stature,
undulating fragrance.
Plant by plant
I will understand the earth,
step by step
as far as the crazy edge
of the ocean.
Suddenly a wave of
air stirs and shakes
wild barley:
a bird
from my feet starts
up abruptly,
earth
a mesh of golden threads
and nameless petals,
glittering sudden as a green rose
entangled in the nettle revealing
its hostile coral snake,
willowy stalks, starry
brambles,
the infinite variety
of each plant that greets me
at times like the rapid
dazzle of thorns
or pulsations of perfume
fresh, subtle and bitter.
Walking toward the spindrift
of the Pacific,

de la primavera escondida,
parece
que antes de que la tierra se termine
cien metros antes del más grande océano
todo se hizo delirio,
germinación y canto.
Las minúsculas hierbas
se coronaron de oro,
las plantas de la arena
dieron rayos morados
y a cada pequeña hoja de olvido
llegó una dirección de luna o fuego.
Cerca del mar, andando,
en el mes de noviembre,
entre los matorrales que reciben
luz, fuego y sal marinas
hallé una flor azul
nacida en la durísima pradera.
De dónde, de qué fondo
tu rayo azul extraes?
Tu seda temblorosa
debajo de la tierra
se comunica con el mar profundo?
La levanté en mis manos
y la miré como si el mar viviera
en una sola gota,
como si el combate
de la tierra y las aguas
una flor levantara
un pequeño estandarte
de fuego azul, de paz irresistible,
de indómita pureza.

clumsily crushing the plants
around a hidden spring,
it seemed that
before earth ends
a hundred yards from the greatest ocean
everything became a delirium
of germination and song.
The miniscule grasses
were crowning with gold,
the plants in the sand
were emanating lavender rays,
and for each small leaf of oblivion
instructions came from fire or the moon.
Close to the sea, walking
in the month of November,
among thickets receiving
fire, salt, and light,
I discovered a seablue flower
blooming in the harshest meadow.
From where, from what depth
do you extract your blue radiance?
Does your silk trembling
below the earth
commune with the depths of the sea?
My hands lifted it up
and I gazed as if the sea
were alive
in that single drop,
as if amid the struggle
of the earth and the waters
one flower were to raise
a small banner
of blue flame, of irresistible peace,
of indomitable purity.

---

* In the Southern hemisphere, November is equivalent to the Northern
hemisphere's May.

Oda a la intranquilidad

Madre intranquilidad, bebí en tus senos
electrizada leche,
acción severa!
No me enseñó la luna
el movimiento.
Es la intranquilidad la que sostiene
el estático vuelo
de la nave,
la sacudida del motor decide
la suavidad del ala
y la miel dormiría en la corola
sin la inquietud insigne de la abeja.
Yo no quiero escaparme
a soledad ninguna.
Yo no quiero
que mis palabras aten a los hombres.
Yo no quiero
mar sin marea, poesía
sin hombre,
pintura
deshabitada, música
sin viento!
Intranquila es la noche
y su hermosura,
todo palpita bajo
sus banderas
y el sol
es encendido movimiento,
ráfaga de alegría!
Se pudren en la charca
las estrellas,
y canta en la cascada
la pureza!

Ode to Restlessness

Mother Restlessness, from your breasts
I have suckled the milk electric,
rash act! It's not the moon
who instilled in me
such commotion.
It is restlessness that jumpstarts
the stalled launch
of a ship,
the agitation of the engine that determines
the thrum of propeller
and without the renowned restlessness of the drone
honey would slumber forever in the corolla.
I've no desire to escape
to some solitude.
Nor do I want
men to be ruled by my words,
I don't wish
for a sea without tides, poetry
without people,
vacant
paintings or music
without the wind!
Restless is the night,
restless its beauty,
everything under its banners
throbbing,
and the sun
an incandescent motion,
a gust of joy!
Stars rot
in standing water
just as purity sings
in the waterfall!

La razón intranquila
inauguró los mares,
y del desorden hizo
nacer el edificio.
No es inmutable
la ciudad, ni tu vida
adquirió la materia de la muerte.
Viajero, ven conmigo.
Daremos
magnitud a los dones de la tierra.
Cambiaremos la espiga.
Llevaremos la luz al más remoto
corazón castigado.
Yo creo
que bajo la intranquila primavera
la claridad
del fruto
se consume,
se extiende
el desarrollo del aroma,
combate el movimiento con la muerte.
Y así llega a tu boca la dulzura
de los frutos gloriosos,
la victoria
de la luz intranquila
que levanta los labios de la tierra.

Out of tumultuous forces
sprang the seas,
the same forces causing buildings to rise up
out of chaos.
The city is not immutable,
nor need your life
be built out of death stuff.
Come with me, traveler.
We'll proclaim the grandeur
of these earthly gifts.
We'll transform the fields of grain.
To the most remote darkened heart
we'll carry light.
I believe
that under the restless spring
even as brilliant
fruit
is consumed
it extends
the circling reach of its scent,
fighting death with that thrust.
And so it happens
that the sweetness
of such glorious fruits reaches your mouth,
in that victory
 for restless light
as it is raised to your lips of mere earth.

Oda a la malvenida

Planta de mi país, rosa de tierra,
estrella trepadora,
zarza negra,
pétalo de la luna en el océano
que amé con sus desgracias y sus olas,
con sus puñales y sus callejones,
amapola
erizada,
clavel de nácar negro,
por qué
cuando mi copa
desbordò y cuando
mi corazòn cambiò de luto a fuego
cuando no tuve para ti,
para ofrecerte,
lo que toda la vida te esperaba,
entonces
tú llegaste,
cuando letras quemantes
van ardiendo en mi frente,
por qué la línea pura
de mi nupcial contorno
llegò como un anillo
rodando por la tierra?
No debías
de todas y de todas
llegar a mi ventana
como un jazmín tardío.
No eras, oh llama oscura,
la que debiò tocarme
y subir con mi sangre
hasta mi boca.

Ode to the Unwelcome One

Flower of my country, rose of earth,
climbing star,
black briar,
petal of the moon in the ocean
I once loved for all its waves and misfortunes,
its daggers and alleys,
bristly poppy,
carnation of black nacre,
why—
when finally my cup
had overflowed when
my heart had exchanged its mourning for fire,
when I no longer had for you
that whole life you were expecting,
why only then
did you come
even as blazing lyrics
were being forged on my brow?
Why has the pure
line of my nuptial contour
arrived like a ring
rolling around on the ground?
Of all possible you's, you
should not
have come
like a late-blooming jasmine
to my window.
Oh, dark fire, you were not
the one destined to touch me
and rise with my blood
up to my mouth.

Ahora
qué puedo contestarte?
Consúmete,
no esperes,
no hay espera
para tus labios de piedra nocturna.
Consúmete,
tú en tu llama,
yo en mi fuego,
y ámame
por el amor que no pudo esperarte,
ámame en lo que tú y yo
tenemos de piedra o de planta:
seguiremos viviendo
de lo que no nos dimos:
del hombro en que no pudo reclinarse una rosa,
de una flor que su propia quemadura ilumina.

Now
how can I answer you?
Consume yourself,
don't wait,
there's no waiting now
for your lips of moonstone.
Consume yourself,
you in your flame,
I in mine,
and love me
for the love that could not wait for you,
love me for what you and I contain
of blossom or stone:
we will always draw life
from all we did not share:
the shoulder upon which a rose could find no peace,
the flower consumed in its own burning.

Oda a los números

Qué sed
de saber cuánto!
Qué hambre
de saber
cuántas
estrellas tiene el cielo!

Nos pasamos
la infancia
contando piedras, plantas,
dedos, arenas, dientes,
la juventud contando
pétalos, cabelleras.
Contamos
los colores, los años,
las vidas y los besos,
en el campo
los bueyes, en el mar
las olas. Los navíos
se hicieron cifras que se fecundaban.
Los números parían.
Las ciudades
eran miles, millones,
el trigo centenares
de unidades que adentro
tenían otros números pequeños,
más pequeños que un grano.
El tiempo se hizo número.
La luz fue numerada
y por más que corrió con el sonido
fue su velocidad un 37.
Nos rodearon los números.

Ode to Numbers

Such a thirst
to know so much!
Such a hunger
to know
how many
stars has the sky!

We spent
our infancy
counting stones, plants,
fingers, sand grains, teeth,
passed our youths counting
petals, comets trails.
We count
colors and years,
life spans and kisses,
bulls
in the fields, waves
in the sea. Ships
became ciphers which multiplied.
Numbers spawned.
Cities
were thousands, millions,
and wheat came in hundreds
of units
each holding other integers
tinier than a single grain.
Time became a number.
Light became numbered
and however much it raced with sound
it had a velocity of 37.
Numbers surrounded us.

Cerrábamos la puerta,
de noche, fatigados,
llegaba un 800,
por debajo,
hasta entrar con nosotros en la cama,
y en el sueño
los 4000 y los 77
picándonos la frente
con sus martillos o sus alicates.
Los 5
agregándose
hasta entrar en el mar o en el delirio,
hasta que el sol saluda con su cero
y nos vamos corriendo
a la oficina,
al taller,
a la fábrica,
a comenzar de nuevo el infinito
número 1 de cada día.

Tuvimos, hombre, tiempo
para que nuestra sed
fuera saciándose,
el ancestral deseo
de enumerar las cosas
y sumarlas,
de reducirlas hasta
hacerlas polvo,
arenales de números.
Fuimos
empapelando el mundo
con números y nombres,
pero
las cosas existían,
se fugaban
del número,
enloquecían en sus cantidades,

When we shut the door
at night, exhausted,
an 800
often slid under the door
and came to bed with us,
and during sleep
the 4,000s and the 77s
pecked at our foreheads with hammers
and nibbled with pliers.
5s
joined 5s
until they entered the sea or delirium,
until the sun saluted us with its zero
and we raced
to the office,
to the workshop,
the factory,
to start all over with the infinite
number 1 of each day.

We had, as men, time
so our thirst could
slowly be satisfied,
the ancestral longing
to enumerate things
and sum them up,
to render them
into dust,
dunes of numbers.
We went on papering
the world
with numbers and names,
but things persisted
fleeing
all numbers,
being driven mad by such quantities,

se evaporaban
dejando
su olor o su recuerdo
y se quedaban los números vacíos.

Por eso,
para ti
quiero las cosas.
Los números
que se vayan a la cárcel,
que se muevan
en columnas cerradas
procreando
hasta darnos la suma
de la totalidad de infinito.
Para ti sólo quiero
que aquellos
números del camino
te defiendan
y que tú los defiendas.
La cifra semanal de tu salario
se desarrolle hasta cubrir tu pecho.
Y del número 2 en que se enlazan
tu cuerpo y el de la mujer amada
salgan los ojos pares de tus hijos
a contar otra vez
las antiguas estrellas
y las innumerables
espigas
que llenarán la tierra transformada.

they vaporized
leaving
their odor or memory,
and leaving the numbers
mere husks.

That is why
for you
I want things.
Let numbers
go to jail,
let them move
in closed columns
procreating
until they give us the sum
for the whole of infinity.
For your sake I only want
those numbers along the way
to defend you
and you to defend them.
May your weekly salary stretch
wide as your chest!
And out of the 2 of you, conjoined,
your body, your beloved's,
may pairs of your children's eyes appear
to tally yet again
ancient stars
and the innumerable
spikes of wheat
by which this transfigured earth
will once again be made complete.

Oda a los poetas populares

Poetas naturales de la tierra,
escondidos en surcos,
cantando en las esquinas,
ciegos de callejón, oh trovadores
de las praderas y los almacenes,
si al agua
comprendiéramos
tal vez como vosotros hablaría,
si las piedras
dijeran su lamento
o su silencio,
con vuestra voz, hermanos,
hablarían.
Numerosos
sois, como las raíces.
En el antiguo corazón
del pueblo
habéis nacido
y de allí viene
vuestra voz sencilla.
Tenéis la jerarquía
del silencioso cántaro de greda
perdido en los rincones,
de pronto canta
cuando se desborda
y es sencillo
su canto,
es sólo tierra y agua.

Así quiero que canten
mis poemas,
que lleven
tierra y agua,

Ode to the Poets of the People

Natural poets of the earth,
hidden in furrows,
singing about street corners
and blind alleys, you bards
of warehouses and prairies—
if we could understand
the waters
perhaps the waters
would speak like you,
if stones could declare their sorrow
or silence
they would speak, brothers,
with your voices.
But what a multitude
you are, like the roots.
From the ancient heart
of a people
you are born
and it's from there you
come by your voices.
Yours is the hierarchy
of the quiet pitcher of white clay
unseen in the corners,
which suddenly sings out
when it overflows
and it is so simple,
its song,
only earth and water.

And just so I wish
my poems to sing,
to carry
earth and water,

fertilidad y canto,
a todo el mundo.
Por eso,
poetas
de mi pueblo,
saludo
la antigua luz que sale
de la tierra.
El eterno
hilo en que se juntaron
pueblo
y
poesía,
nunca
se cortó
este profundo
hilo de piedra,
viene
desde tan lejos
como
la memoria
del hombre.
Vio
con los ojos ciegos
de los vates
nacer la tumultuosa
primavera,
la sociedad humana,
el primer beso,
y en la guerra
cantó sobre la sangre,
allí estaba mi hermano
barba roja,
cabeza ensangrentada
y ojos ciegos,
con su lira,

fecundity and song,
to the whole world.
That is why,
poets
of my people,
I salute
the ancient light flowing
from the earth.
The eternal thread
by which people
and
poetry
are joined,
it was never
cut,
this profound
thread of stone,
come
from as far
as the
memory
of man.
It has witnessed with
the blind eyes
of poets
the birth of
tumultuous
spring, human society,
the first kiss;
in war
it sang over the blood,
and there, then, was my brother,
beard red,
head bloodied
and eyes blind;
with his lyre

allí estaba
cantando
entre los muertos,
Homero
se llamaba
o Pastor Pérez,
o Reinaldo Donoso.
Sus endechas
eran allí y ahora
un vuelo blanco,
una paloma,
eran la paz, la rama
del árbol del aceite,
y la continuidad de la hermosura.
Más tarde
los absorbió la calle,
la campiña,
los encontré cantando
entre las reses,
en la celebración
del desafío,
relatando las penas
de los pobres,
llevando las noticias
de las inundaciones,
detallando las ruinas
del incendio
o la noche nefanda
de los asesinatos.

Ellos,
los poetas
de mi pueblo,
errantes,
pobres entre los pobres,
sostuvieron
sobre sus canciones

he was there
singing
among the dead,
Homer
was his name
or Pastor Pérez
or Reinaldo Donoso.
His dirges
were there and now
came the white flight
of a dove,
bearing
in the olive twig
peace and the continuity
of beauty. Later,
reabsorbed among streets
and open fields,
I met them singing
among the cattle
in a celebration
of defiance,
telling the trials
of the poor,
carrying news
of floods,
detailing ravages
of fires,
the unspeakable darkness
of assassinations.

These, the poets
of my people,
wandering
poor among the poor,
maintained
a smile
throughout their songs,

la sonrisa,
criticaron con sorna
a los explotadores,
contaron la miseria
del minero
y el destino implacable
del soldado.

Ellos,
los poetas
del pueblo,
con guitarra harapienta
y ojos conocedores
de la vida,
sostuvieron
en su canto
una rosa
y la mostraron en los callejones
para que se supiera
que la vida
no será siempre triste.
Payadores, poetas
humildemente altivos,
a través
de la historia
y sus reveses,
a través
de la paz y de la guerra,
de la noche y la aurora,
sois vosotros
los depositarios,
los tejedores
de la poesía,
y ahora
aquí en mi patria
está el tesoro,
el cristal de Castilla,

ironically judging
exploiters,
relating the misery
of the miner
and the relentless
fate of the soldier.

These,
the poets
of my people,
guitars battered
and eyes skilled
at discerning
what survives,
kept a rose
in their song
and paraded it
through the alleys
so that it would be known
that life
will not always be sad.
Guitarist and singer, poets
proud to be humble
throughout history
and its setbacks,
throughout
peace and war,
darkness and dawn,
your voices
have been the repository,
the warp and woof
of poetry,
and now
here in my homeland
lies the treasure
the crystal of Castille,

la soledad de Chile,
la pícara inocencia,
y la guitarra contra el infortunio,
la mano solidaria
en el camino,
la palabra
repetida en el canto
y transmitida,
la voz de piedra y agua
entre raíces,
la rapsodia del viento,
la voz que no requiere librerías,
todo lo que debemos aprender
los orgullosos:
con la verdad del pueblo
la eternidad del canto.

the solitude of Chile,
the mischievous innocence,
and the guitar strummed against misfortune,
the helping hand
along the way,
the words repeated in song
and passed on,
the voice of stone and water
among roots,
the rhapsody of wind,
the voice with no need for books,
we, the proud, must
learn these words:
From the truth of the people
springs the eternity of song.

Oda a la tristeza

Tristeza, escarabajo
de siete patas rotas,
huevo de telaraña,
rata descalabrada,
esqueleto de perra:
Aquí no entras.
No pasas.
Ándate.
Vuelve
al Sur con tu paraguas,
vuelve
al Norte con tus dientes de culebra.
Aquí vive un poeta.
La tristeza no puede
entrar por estas puertas.
Por las ventanas
entra el aire del mundo,
las rojas rosas nuevas,
las banderas bordadas
del pueblo y sus victorias.
No puedes.
Aquí no entras.
Sacude
tus alas de murciélago,
yo pisaré las plumas
que caen de tu manto,
yo barreré los trozos
de tu cadáver hacia
las cuatro puntas del viento,
yo te torceré el cuello,
te coseré los ojos,
cortaré tu mortaja
y enterraré tus huesos roedores
bajo la primavera de un manzano.

Ode to Gloom

Gloom, you scarab
of seven broken legs,
you cobweb's egg,
scramble-brained rat,
skeleton of a bitch:
Don't come in here.
Don't bother to stop.
Walk right on by.
Go back
south with your umbrella,
go back
north with your serpent's teeth.
Here lives a poet.
Gloom cannot
trudge in through these doors.
Through these windows
blow the breezes of the world,
the roses red and fresh,
the flags embroidered
by the people and their victories.
Not you.
Don't come in here.
Beat your bat wings,
and I will tromp on the plumes
that fall from your cloak.
I will sweep every scrap
of your sorry carcass
to the four corners of the wind,
I'll wring your neck,
stitch your eyes shut,
cut out your shroud,
and I will bury you, Gloom,
I will sink your rat-gnawed bones deep
under the spring of a blossoming apple tree.

Oda a la pobreza

Cuando nací,
pobreza,
me seguiste,
me mirabas
a través
de las tablas podridas
por el profundo invierno.
De pronto
eran tus ojos
los que miraban desde los agujeros.
Las goteras,
de noche, repetían
tu nombre y apellido
o a veces
el salto quebrado, el traje roto,
los zapatos abiertos,
me advertían.
Allí estabas
acechándome
tus dientes de carcoma,
tus ojos de pantano,
tu lengua gris
que corta
la ropa, la madera,
los huesos y la sangre,
allí estabas
buscándome,
siguiéndome,
desde mi nacimiento
por las calles.

Cuando alquilé una pieza
pequeña, en los suburbios,

Ode to Poverty

When I was born,
Poverty,
you followed me,
you would look at me
aslant
through the rotten slats
of deep winter.
Suddenly
they were your eyes
the ones that would look
from the holes.
The drips,
at night, repeated
your first and last names
and sometimes
the bankrupt wit, the torn suit,
the shoes split wide open,
were warning me.
There you were
waiting for me
like gnawing teeth,
your eyes swampy,
your grey blade of a tongue
cut clothing, wood,
bones, blood,
there you were
looking for me,
stalking me
through the streets
ever since I was born.

When I rented a small
room in the suburbs,

sentada en una silla
me esperabas,
o al descorrer las sábanas
en un hotel oscuro,
adolescente,
no encontré la fragancia
de la rosa desnuda,
sino el silbido frío
de tu boca.
Pobreza,
me seguiste
por los cuarteles y los hospitales,
por la paz y la guerra.
Cuando enfermé tocaron
a la puerta:
no era el doctor, entraba
otra vez la pobreza.
Te vi sacar mis muebles
a la calle:
los hombres
los dejaban caer como pedradas.
Tú, con amor horrible,
de un montón de abandono
en medio de la calle y de la lluvia
ibas haciendo
un trono desdentado
y mirando a los pobres
recogías
mi último plato haciéndolo diadema.
Ahora,
pobreza,
yo te sigo.
Como fuiste implacable,
soy implacable.
Junto
a cada pobre

seated in a chair
you waited for me,
and when I drew the curtains back
in a hotel, dark,
adolescent,
I wasn't met with the fragrance
of the naked rose,
only the cold hiss
from your lips.
Poverty,
you followed me
through barracks and hospitals,
through peace and war.
When I fell ill, a knock
at the door:
It wasn't the doctor; Poverty
entered again.
I watched you take my furniture out
to the street :
The men
let it all fall like thrown stones.
You, with horrible love,
from a heap of discards
in the middle of the street and the rain
were making
a toothless throne
and looking at the poor
you would take back
my last dish
making of it a diadem.
Now,
Poverty,
I follow you.
As you were relentless
I am relentless.
Alongside
every poor person

me encontrarás cantando,
bajo
cada sábana
de hospital imposible
encontrarás mi canto.
Te sigo,
pobreza,
te vigilo,
te acerco,
te disparo,
te aíslo,
te cerceno las uñas,
te rompo
los dientes que te quedan.
Estoy
en todas partes:
en el océano con los pescadores,
en la mina
los hombres
al limpiarse la frente,
secarse el sudor negro,
encuentran
mis poemas.
Yo salgo cada día
con la obrera textil.
Tengo las manos blancas
de dar pan en las panaderías.
Donde vayas,
pobreza,
mi canto
está cantando,
mi vida
está viviendo,
mi sangre
está luchando.

you will find me singing,
under
every hospital sheet
you will run into my song.
I follow you,
Poverty,
I watch you,
I approach,
I open fire,
I isolate you,
I cut your claws,
I tear out the teeth
you have left.
I am
everywhere:
In the ocean with the fishermen,
in the mines
where men
wipe their foreheads,
drying their black sweat,
they encounter
my poems.
I go out everyday
with the textile worker.
I have white hands
from giving out loaves at the bakery.
Where you go,
Poverty,
my song
is being sung,
my life
is being lived,
my blood
is struggling.

Derrotaré
tus pálidas banderas
en donde se levanten.

Otros poetas
antaño te llamaron
santa,
veneraron tu capa,
se alimentaron de humo
y desaparecieron.
Yo te desafío,
con duros versos te golpeo el rostro,
te embarco y te destierro.
Yo con otros,
con otros, muchos otros,
te vamos expulsando
de la tierra a la luna
para que allí te quedes
fría y encarcelada
mirando con un ojo
el pan y los racimos
que cubrirá la tierra
de mañana.

I trample
your pale flags
wherever they are raised.

Other poets
in times past called you
Saint,
they venerated your cloak,
they fed upon vapors
and they vanished.
I defy you,
with tough verses I batter your face,
I deport you and I exile you.
I with others,
yes others, many others,
we are going to banish you
from earth to the moon
so that there you remain
cold and incarcerated
watching with one eye
the loaves and clusters of fruit
that will cloak the earth
tomorrow.

Oda al vino

Vino color de día,
vino color de noche,
vino con pies de púrpura
o sangre de topacio,
vino,
estrellado hijo
de la tierra,
vino, liso
como una espada de oro,
suave
como un desordenado terciopelo,
vino encaracolado
y suspendido,
amoroso,
marino,
nunca has cabido en una copa,
en un canto, en un hombre,
coral, gregario eres,
y cuando menos, mutuo.
A veces
te nutres de recuerdos
mortales,
en tu ola
vamos de tumba en tumba,
picapedrero de sepulcro helado,
y lloramos
lágrimas transitorias,
pero
tu hermoso
traje de primavera
es diferente,
el corazón sube a las ramas,
el viento mueve el día,
nada queda

Ode to Wine

Wine the color of day,
color of night,
wine with purple feet
or topaz blood,
wine,
star-child
of earth,
wine smooth
as a golden sword,
gentle
as rumpled velvet,
encased in the swirl-shell
of snail,
amorous, marine,
there's never room for you in one cup,
one song, one man;
you are choral, gregarious,
reciprocal, to say the least.
At times
you feed on deadly
memories,
and on your wave
we go from grave to grave,
carver of an icy sepulcher,
and we weep
our transitory tears,
but
your beautiful
spring dress
is quite another matter,
heart rises through the limbs,
wind moves the day,
nothing remains

dentro de tu alma inmóvil.
El vino
mueve la primavera,
crece como una planta la alegría,
caen muros,
peñascos,
se cierran los abismos,
nace el canto.
Oh tú, jarra de vino, en el desierto
con la sabrosa que amo,
dijo el viejo poeta.
Que el cántaro de vino
al beso del amor sume su beso.

Amor mio, de pronto
tu cadera
es la curva colmada
de la copa,
tu pecho es el racimo,
la luz del alcohol tu cabellera,
las uvas tus pezones,
tu ombligo sello puro
estampado en tu vientre de vasija,
y tu amor la cascada
de vino inextinguible,
la claridad que cae en mis sentidos,
el esplendor terrestre de la vida.

Pero no sólo amor,
beso quemante
o corazón quemado
eres, vino de vida,
sino
amistad de los seres, transparencia,
coro de disciplina,
abundancia de flores.

in your stilled soul.
Wine
stirs spring,
swells like vegetal joy,
walls fall back
and great stones,
chasms are sealed
as song is born.
The ancient poet said,
Oh you, jug of wine, in the wilderness,
and I with my sweetheart, my beloved.
Thus does the flowing wine
add to the kiss of love
a kiss of its own.

My love, your hip
suddenly
is the brimming curve
of the wine glass,
your breast is the cluster,
your long tresses luminous with spirits,
your nipples the grapes,
your navel the virgin seal stamped
upon the vessel of your belly,
and your love is the cascade
of inextinguishable wine,
the clarity that illuminates my senses,
the terrestrial splendor of life.

But you are not only love,
the sear of a kiss
or the blazing heart,
more than the wine of life,
for you are also the companionship
of essences, transparency,
the choir of discipline,
the multitudinous flowers.

Amo sobre una mesa,
cuando se habla,
la luz de una botella
de inteligente vino.
Que lo beban,
que recuerden en cada
gota de oro
o copa de topacio
o cuchara de púrpura
que trabajó el otoño
hasta llenar de vino las vasijas
y aprenda el hombre oscuro,
en el ceremonial de su negocio,
a recordar la tierra y sus deberes,
a propagar el cántico del fruto.

I love it when at table,
where we are talking,
the brilliance from a bottle
of vintner's genius flashes forth.
Drink,
and remember in each
drop of gold
or cup of topaz
or spoonful of purple
how autumn worked
to fill the vessels with wine,
and through the rituals of his concerns
let the unsung man learn
how to remember the earth and his obligations,
how to propagate the canticle of the grape.

Wilⅼiam Pitt Root's numerous poetry collections include *The Storm and Other Poems, Reasons For Going It On Foot, Faultdancing* and *Trace Elements from a Recurring Kingdom: The First Five Books of William Pitt Root.* Honors accorded his poetry, which appears in *The Atlantic, New Yorker, The Nation,* and *Poetry,* include grants from the Rockefeller and Guggenheim Foundations, and the National Endowment for the Arts; a Stegner Fellowship at Stanford and a United States/United Kingdom Exchange Artist Fellowship. Root's work, published in twenty languages, has won the Stanley Kunitz Prize and Guy Owen awards, and three Pushcart Prizes.

Root's academic career includes periods at Hunter College–CUNY, the University of Montana, Amherst College, Interlochen Arts Academy, New York University, and Distinguished Visiting Writer residencies at Pacific Lutheran and Wichita State Universities. Most recently he has served as the John C. Hodges visiting writer at the University of Tennessee, Knoxville. He and his wife, poet Pamela Uschuk, live primarily in the West with a cadre of four-legged companions and enjoy traveling widely to teach and read from their works at home and abroad.

As a child growing up where the Everglades met the Gulf of Mexico, Root often smuggled a radio into his bed nights so he could hear the late night Spanish broadcasts from Havana. "That music came from a part of the universe where people knew how to live their lives far more passionately than anyone I'd ever met. I was mesmerized and heartened by all that energy, all that poetry, as a kid. I still am."

Acknowledgments

Many of these translations first appeared in slightly different versions in the following periodicals and anthologies: *Anthology and Yearbook of Magazine Verse, Asheville Poetry Review, CutBank, Historical Mathematics Network Journal, International Virtual Institute for Historical Studies of Mathematics, Mississippi Mud, The Proud Word,* and *Telescope.*

Colophon

This first edition of *Sublime Blue: Selected Early
Odes of Pablo Neruda*, translated by William
Pitt Root, has been printed on 55 pound
Edwards Brothers Natural Paper containing a
high percentage of recycled fiber. Titles have
been set in Colonna MT type, the text in Adobe
Caslon type. All Wings Press books are
designed and produced by Bryce Milligan.

On-line catalogue and ordering:
www.wingspress.com

Wings Press titles are distributed
to the trade by the
Independent Publishers Group
www.ipgbook.com
and in Europe by
www.gazellebookservices.co.uk

Also available as an ebook.